★ THE ★
UNITED
STATES
PRESIDENTS

CALVIN
COOLIDGE

Heidi M.D. Elston

**Checkerboard
Library**

An Imprint of Abdo Publishing
abdobooks.com

ABDOBOOKS.COM

Published by Abdo Publishing, a division of ABDO, PO Box 398166, Minneapolis, Minnesota 55439. Copyright © 2021 by Abdo Consulting Group, Inc. International copyrights reserved in all countries. No part of this book may be reproduced in any form without written permission from the publisher. Checkerboard Library™ is a trademark and logo of Abdo Publishing.

Printed in the United States of America, North Mankato, Minnesota
052020
092020

THIS BOOK CONTAINS
RECYCLED MATERIALS

Design: Emily O'Malley, Kelly Doudna, Mighty Media, Inc.
Production: Mighty Media, Inc.
Editor: Liz Salzmann

Cover Photograph: Stock Montage/Getty Images
Interior Photographs: Albert de Bruijn/iStockphoto, p. 37; AP Images, pp. 6 (young Coolidge), 10, 11, 14, 23, 36; The Crowley Company/Library of Congress, p. 28; General Photographic Agency/Getty Images, p. 32; Getty Images, pp. 17, 18, 19, 26, 27, 31; Hulton Archive/Getty Images, pp. 5, 15; Kenneth C. Zirkel/Wikimedia Commons, p. 7; Keystone/Getty Images, p. 25; Lee Snider/Getty Images, p. 33; Library of Congress, pp. 6, 7 (Warren G. Harding), 20, 40; New York Times Co./Getty Images, p. 13; Pete Souza/Flickr, p. 44; Popperfoto/Getty Images, pp. 12, 21; Shutterstock Images, pp. 38, 39; Wikimedia Commons, pp. 7 (Coolidge in chair), 29, 40 (George Washington), 42

Library of Congress Control Number: 2019956445

Publisher's Cataloging-in-Publication Data
Names: Elston, Heidi M.D., author.
Title: Calvin Coolidge / by Heidi M.D. Elston
Description: Minneapolis, Minnesota : Abdo Publishing, 2021 | Series: The United States presidents | Includes online resources and index.
Identifiers: ISBN 9781532193460 (lib. bdg.) | ISBN 9781098212100 (ebook)
Subjects: LCSH: Coolidge, Calvin, 1872-1933--Juvenile literature. | Presidents--Biography--Juvenile literature. | Presidents--United States--History--Juvenile literature. | Legislators--United States—Biography--Juvenile literature. | Politics and government--Biography--Juvenile literature.
Classification: DDC 973.915092--dc23

★ CONTENTS ★

Calvin Coolidge

Calvin Coolidge became the thirtieth US president in 1923. During the 1920s, the US **economy** was strong. The **stock market** was booming. Most people had good jobs and owned their own homes and cars. Many Americans called these good times "Coolidge prosperity."

Americans praised President Coolidge for their good fortune. But shortly after he left office, it all came crumbling down. In 1929, the country's economy failed. This led to the **Great Depression**.

Before becoming president, Coolidge served as a state representative and a state senator. He became lieutenant governor and then governor. Coolidge worked hard for the citizens he represented.

In 1921, Coolidge became vice president of the United States. Two years later, President Warren G. Harding died while in office. Coolidge was next in line to be president.

Vice President Coolidge took the oath of office and became president. As president, Coolidge was honest and hardworking. He did what he thought was best for Americans.

TIMELINE

1872

On July 4, John Calvin Coolidge was born in Plymouth, Vermont.

1897

Coolidge became a lawyer.

1905

On October 4, Coolidge married Grace Anna Goodhue.

1909

Coolidge was elected to his first term as mayor of Northampton.

1895

Coolidge graduated from Amherst College in Amherst, Massachusetts.

1898

In Massachusetts, Coolidge was elected to the Northampton City Council.

1906

Coolidge was elected to the Massachusetts House of Representatives.

1911

Coolidge was elected to the Massachusetts state senate.

1919

Coolidge took office as governor of Massachusetts on January 1. Later, he helped end the Boston Police Strike.

1923

President Harding died on August 2. On August 3, Coolidge became the thirtieth US president.

1927

Coolidge announced he would not seek reelection.

1933

On January 5, Calvin Coolidge died.

1916

On January 6, Coolidge became lieutenant governor of Massachusetts.

1921

On March 4, Coolidge became vice president of the United States under Warren G. Harding.

1925

On March 4, Coolidge was inaugurated as president.

1929

Coolidge signed the Kellogg-Briand Pact.

" The right thing to do ...

is always simple and direct."

CALVIN COOLIDGE

DID YOU KNOW?

★ Calvin Coolidge loved animals. He even owned a pet raccoon that he walked on a leash! Her name was Rebecca.

★ In 1923, President Coolidge lit the first national Christmas tree on the White House lawn.

★ On March 4, 1925, Chief Justice William Taft of the US Supreme Court gave the oath of office to Coolidge. That day, Taft became the first former president to give the presidential oath.

★ Coolidge was a quiet man. Once, a woman bet she could get more than two words out of him. When she told Coolidge this he replied, "You lose."

★ On August 10, 1927, President Coolidge attended the formal dedication of Mount Rushmore in South Dakota. There, Coolidge gave a speech and promised federal funding for the monument.

Young Calvin

John Calvin Coolidge was born in Plymouth, Vermont, on July 4, 1872. His parents were John Calvin and Victoria Moor Coolidge. They called their son Calvin to avoid confusion. Calvin had a younger sister named Abigail. She was his closest friend.

John was a farmer and a storekeeper. He was also active in local politics. Victoria loved poetry. She taught Calvin and Abigail to read. When Calvin was only 12 years old, his mother died. Calvin was deeply saddened.

★ FAST FACTS

BORN: July 4, 1872

WIFE: Grace Anna Goodhue (1879–1957)

CHILDREN: 2

POLITICAL PARTY: Republican

AGE AT INAUGURATION: 51

YEARS SERVED: 1923–1929

VICE PRESIDENT: Charles Dawes

DIED: January 5, 1933, age 60

Seven-year-old Calvin

Calvin (*standing, second from left*) with his graduating class at Black River Academy

Young Calvin helped his father on the farm. He drove the mowing machine, tended cattle, and planted potatoes. Calvin also had time to play and have fun. He skated, sledded, and took hayrides in the winter. In the summer Calvin loved to fish, swim, and ride horses.

Calvin attended Black River Academy in Ludlow, Vermont. His favorite subjects were Latin and history. Shortly before his graduation in 1890, Abigail died. Again, Calvin was heartbroken.

Entering Politics

In 1891, Coolidge entered Amherst College in Amherst, Massachusetts. He graduated in 1895 and moved to Northampton, Massachusetts. There, he studied law at the Hammond and Field law firm. Coolidge became a lawyer in 1897. About seven months later, he opened a law office in Northampton.

During this time, Coolidge became active in the **Republican** Party. In 1898, he was elected to the Northampton City Council. Two years later, Coolidge became the city solicitor, or lawyer. He was reelected to this position the next year.

In Northampton, Coolidge met a young woman named Grace Anna Goodhue. Grace had been born in Burlington, Vermont. She taught at the Clarke School for the Deaf in Northampton.

Grace Coolidge

12

The Coolidge family

Coolidge was shy and quiet, but Grace was the opposite. She was warm and outgoing. The two married on October 4, 1905. They shared a loving relationship. Soon, the Coolidges had two sons. John was born in 1906. Calvin Jr. followed in 1908.

Rising in Politics

Meanwhile, **Coolidge was still active in politics.** But he wasn't like most politicians. He rarely smiled. And, he didn't flatter people to get their votes. Coolidge was smart and trustworthy. People liked his honesty.

In 1906, Coolidge was elected to the Massachusetts House of Representatives. There, he fought for the rights of workers and women. Coolidge reduced working hours, and he supported women's right to vote. He won reelection the next year.

— Young Coolidge —

In 1909, Coolidge was elected mayor of Northampton. He increased wages for teachers and helped lower taxes. The next year, he won reelection.

Coolidge was elected to the Massachusetts state senate in 1911. As a senator, Coolidge was chairman of the Committee on Legal Affairs and the Committee on Agriculture. Coolidge also helped resolve a strike at the

The Coolidges lived in the left half
of this duplex in Northampton.

American Woolen Company. Later, he served as senate
president for two terms.

Next, Coolidge ran for lieutenant governor of
Massachusetts. He won the election in 1915 and took office
on January 6, 1916. As lieutenant governor, Coolidge
delivered speeches on local and state issues. He was
reelected to this position twice.

Governor Coolidge

In 1918, Coolidge ran for governor of Massachusetts. He narrowly won the election. Coolidge took office on January 1, 1919.

Governor Coolidge soon won national attention for his role in the Boston Police Strike. That year, more than 1,100 of the 1,500 city police officers went on strike. Two days of disorder followed. Then, Governor Coolidge called in the state guard to control the city.

Police Commissioner Edwin U. Curtis decided the striking officers would lose their jobs. He said they had abandoned their jobs by going on strike. Labor leader Samuel Gompers protested this decision. He wanted the strikers to get their jobs back.

But Governor Coolidge agreed with Curtis. "There is no right to strike against the public safety by anybody, anywhere, anytime," Coolidge said. People across the country praised the governor for his tough stand. That year, he was reelected by a record vote.

During the Boston Police Strike, eight city residents were killed. More than 20 were seriously wounded.

Death of a President

In 1920, **Republican** Party leaders nominated Warren G. Harding to run for president. They chose Coolidge to run for vice president. Harding faced off against **Democratic** governor James M. Cox of Ohio. Cox's **running mate** was Assistant Secretary of the Navy Franklin D. Roosevelt.

The 1920 election marked the first time women could vote. In the past, Harding and Coolidge had each fought for women's rights. Women remembered this support and voted for them. This helped Harding and Coolidge win the race.

Harding–Coolidge campaign button

Harding was **inaugurated** as the twenty-ninth US president on March 4, 1921. That day, Coolidge became vice president. As vice president, Coolidge was in charge of the US Senate. He controlled **debates** and

Never before in US history had a president been sworn in by his father.

managed the senators. Coolidge also attended President Harding's **cabinet** meetings.

In summer 1923, Coolidge visited his father in Vermont. One night, Coolidge was awoken with some shocking news. President Harding had died. At 2:47 a.m. on August 3, Coolidge was sworn into office by his father, a **notary public**. Then, he turned out the lights and went back to bed.

Cleaning House

Harding's **administration** had been filled with many **dishonest people.** Other government officials feared they were taking bribes and lying to the nation.

President Coolidge hired two lawyers to conduct investigations. They brought to court anyone involved in political crimes. Americans liked President Coolidge's swift action and firm leadership. He restored the country's trust in government.

Coolidge continued Harding's policy of supporting US businesses. He kept **tariffs** high to help American manufacturers. He also reduced income taxes and kept government spending low. As a result, President Coolidge reduced the national **debt** by about $1 billion a year.

Warren G. Harding

President Coolidge worked hard to quickly remove all dishonesty from the White House.

PRESIDENT COOLIDGE'S CABINET

FIRST TERM

August 3, 1923–March 4, 1925

- ★ **STATE:** Charles Evans Hughes
- ★ **TREASURY:** Andrew W. Mellon
- ★ **WAR:** John Wingate Weeks
- ★ **NAVY:** Edwin Denby
  Curtis Dwight Wilbur (from March 18, 1924)
- ★ **ATTORNEY GENERAL:** Harry Micajah Daugherty
  Harlan Fiske Stone (from April 9, 1924)
- ★ **INTERIOR:** Hubert Work
- ★ **AGRICULTURE:** Henry Cantwell Wallace
  Howard Mason Gore (from November 21, 1924)
- ★ **COMMERCE:** Herbert Hoover
- ★ **LABOR:** James John Davis

SECOND TERM

March 4, 1925–March 4, 1929

- ★ **STATE:** Frank B. Kellogg
- ★ **TREASURY:** Andrew W. Mellon
- ★ **WAR:** John Wingate Weeks
  Dwight F. Davis (from October 14, 1925)
- ★ **NAVY:** Curtis Dwight Wilbur
- ★ **ATTORNEY GENERAL:** John Garibaldi Sargent
- ★ **INTERIOR:** Hubert Work
  Roy Owen West (from January 21, 1929)
- ★ **AGRICULTURE:** William Marion Jardine
- ★ **COMMERCE:** Herbert Hoover
  William Fairfield Whiting (from December 11, 1928)
- ★ **LABOR:** James John Davis

Coolidge (*seated, third from left*) with his cabinet in 1927

"Keep Cool with Coolidge"

Tragedy soon struck the Coolidge family. In 1924, 16-year-old Calvin Jr. died of a foot **infection**. Coolidge suffered from the loss of his son. He said, "When he went, the power and the glory of the presidency went with him."

Coolidge was tired and sad. Yet he entered the 1924 election for president. Bureau of the Budget director Charles Dawes was his **running mate**.

The **Democrats** chose John W. Davis of West Virginia to run for president. Nebraska governor Charles W. Bryan was his running mate.

Unhappy **Republicans** and Democrats formed the **Progressive** Party. They nominated Wisconsin senator Robert M. La Follette for president. Montana senator Burton K. Wheeler was chosen for his running mate. Coolidge campaigned with the **slogan** "Keep Cool with Coolidge." Americans were happy with him, and he easily won the election.

★ **SUPREME COURT APPOINTMENT**

HARLAN FISKE STONE: 1925

Charles Dawes

President Coolidge

Coolidge was **inaugurated** on March 4, 1925. Again, he maintained his firm stand on taxes and government spending. Businesses continued to grow and **stock market** prices rose.

Twice, Congress tried to pass the McNary-Haugen bill. This bill would help farmers get out of **debt**. But Coolidge stopped it both times. He worried the bill would raise prices for consumers. However, the bill could have reduced farmers' problems during the **Great Depression**.

President Coolidge also opposed a bonus bill for soldiers who had fought in **World War I**. Congress passed the bill over him. The Veterans Bonus Act provided these former soldiers with **insurance** policies.

In 1929, Coolidge signed the Kellogg-Briand Pact. This agreement

Kellogg-Briand Pact

President Coolidge signing
the Kellogg-Briand Pact

prevented using war to settle quarrels between countries. Sixty-one other nations also signed the treaty. It is named for US **Secretary of State** Frank B. Kellogg and French foreign minister Aristide Briand.

Coolidge Prosperity

Under President Coolidge's leadership, America's **economy** flourished. Big businesses such as banks grew even larger. Factories shipped huge amounts of goods. Stores opened across the country. And, sales of buildings and land boomed.

The main way Coolidge helped businesses was to keep taxes low. He believed that if business owners paid less in taxes, they would use the extra money to expand their companies. The bigger companies would then provide more jobs.

Secretary of the Treasury Andrew Mellon worked with Coolidge to reduce business taxes.

Coolidge prosperity gave many Americans better lives. Workers enjoyed higher pay and a shorter workweek. However, not everyone benefited from Coolidge prosperity. Nearly 2 million Americans were without jobs. Farmers also suffered greatly. Crop prices fell, and farmers sold less in foreign markets. Still, Coolidge opposed farm relief.

Coolidge's official presidential portrait

Coolidge Goes Home

In 1927, President Coolidge had released a historic statement. He said, "I do not choose to run for president in 1928." The nation had been stunned. Times were good. Why wouldn't he want to be reelected? Coolidge did not explain his decision.

Coolidge left the White House in March 1929 and retired to Northampton. There, he spent time with his family. He also wrote magazine and newspaper articles. And, he wrote a book called The **Autobiography** of Calvin Coolidge.

Coolidge served as a director of the New York Life **Insurance** Company. In addition, he was president of the American Antiquarian Society. This historical society collects and preserves records of the lives and activities of Americans.

For greater privacy, the Coolidges eventually moved to a Northampton estate called The Beeches. There, gates kept tourists at a distance. Coolidge also had plenty of room to walk and play with the family's dogs.

The Coolidges purchased The Beeches in 1930.

Coolidge was known
as "Silent Cal."

In October 1929, the US **economy** failed. **Stock market** prices dropped and banks and other businesses closed. Worst of all, many Americans lost their jobs. This was the beginning of the **Great Depression**.

The depression saddened Coolidge. Most citizens felt that his leadership had failed. While president, many people had praised his leadership. Now, those same people blamed his policies for America's troubles. They felt he could have done more to prevent the economic failure.

On January 5, 1933, Calvin Coolidge died of a heart attack in his home.

Mr. and Mrs. Coolidge are buried
in Plymouth Notch Cemetery.

He was 60 years old. Coolidge was buried in Plymouth
beside his son.

Coolidge was a shy, quiet, sincere man who rarely
smiled. He worked hard for his country and showed strong
leadership. Coolidge believed actions were more powerful
than words. As a result, he earned the respect of voters.
Calvin Coolidge helped Americans trust in government
again.

BRANCHES OF GOVERNMENT

The US government is divided into three branches. They are the executive, legislative, and judicial branches. This division is called a separation of powers. Each branch has some power over the others. This is called a system of checks and balances.

★ EXECUTIVE BRANCH

The executive branch enforces laws. It is made up of the president, the vice president, and the president's cabinet. The president represents the United States around the world. He or she oversees relations with other countries and signs treaties. The president signs bills into law and appoints officials and federal judges. He or she also leads the military and manages government workers.

★ LEGISLATIVE BRANCH

The legislative branch makes laws, maintains the military, and regulates trade. It also has the power to declare war. This branch consists of the Senate and the House of Representatives. Together, these two houses make up Congress. Each state has two senators. A state's population determines the number of representatives it has.

★ JUDICIAL BRANCH

The judicial branch interprets laws. It consists of district courts, courts of appeals, and the Supreme Court. District courts try cases. If a person disagrees with a trial's outcome, he or she may appeal. If a court of appeals supports the ruling, a person may appeal to the Supreme Court. The Supreme Court also makes sure that laws follow the US Constitution.

★ QUALIFICATIONS FOR OFFICE

To be president, a person must meet three requirements. A candidate must be at least 35 years old and a natural-born US citizen. He or she must also have lived in the United States for at least 14 years.

★ ELECTORAL COLLEGE

The US presidential election is an indirect election. Voters from each state choose electors to represent them in the Electoral College. The number of electors from each state is based on the state's population. Each elector has one electoral vote. Electors are pledged to cast their vote for the candidate who receives the highest number of popular votes in their state. A candidate must receive the majority of Electoral College votes to win.

★ TERM OF OFFICE

Each president may be elected to two four-year terms. Sometimes, a president may only be elected once. This happens if he or she served more than two years of the previous president's term.

The presidential election is held on the Tuesday after the first Monday in November. The president is sworn in on January 20 of the following year. At that time, he or she takes the oath of office:

> *I do solemnly swear (or affirm) that I will faithfully execute the office of President of the United States, and will to the best of my ability, preserve, protect and defend the Constitution of the United States.*

The Presidential Succession Act of 1947 defines who becomes president if the president cannot serve. The vice president is first in the line of succession. Next are the Speaker of the House and the President Pro Tempore of the Senate. If none of these individuals is able to serve, the office falls to the president's cabinet members. They would take office in the order in which each department was created:

Secretary of State

Secretary of the Treasury

Secretary of Defense

Attorney General

Secretary of the Interior

Secretary of Agriculture

Secretary of Commerce

Secretary of Labor

Secretary of Health
and Human Services

Secretary of Housing and
Urban Development

Secretary of Transportation

Secretary of Energy

Secretary of Education

Secretary of Veterans Affairs

**Secretary of Homeland
Security**

While in office, the president receives a salary of $400,000 each year. He or she lives in the White House and has 24-hour Secret Service protection.

The president may travel on a Boeing 747 jet called Air Force One. The airplane can accommodate 76 passengers. It has kitchens, a dining room, sleeping areas, and a conference room. It also has fully equipped offices with the latest communications systems. Air Force One can fly halfway around the world before needing to refuel. It can even refuel in flight!

Air Force One

If the president wishes to travel by car, he or she uses Cadillac One. It has been modified with heavy armor and communications systems. The president takes

Cadillac One

Cadillac One along when visiting other countries if secure transportation will be needed.

The president also travels on a helicopter called Marine One. Like the presidential car, Marine One accompanies the president when traveling abroad if necessary.

Sometimes, the president needs to get away and relax with family and friends. Camp David is the official presidential retreat. It is located in the cool, wooded mountains of Maryland. The US Navy maintains the retreat, and the US Marine Corps keeps it secure. The camp offers swimming, tennis, golf, and hiking.

When the president leaves office, he or she receives lifetime Secret Service protection. He or she also receives a yearly pension of $207,800 and funding for office space, supplies, and staff.

Marine One

	PRESIDENT	PARTY	TOOK OFFICE
1	George Washington	None	April 30, 1789
2	John Adams	Federalist	March 4, 1797
3	Thomas Jefferson	Democratic-Republican	March 4, 1801
4	James Madison	Democratic-Republican	March 4, 1809
5	James Monroe	Democratic-Republican	March 4, 1817
6	John Quincy Adams	Democratic-Republican	March 4, 1825
7	Andrew Jackson	Democrat	March 4, 1829
8	Martin Van Buren	Democrat	March 4, 1837
9	William H. Harrison	Whig	March 4, 1841
10	John Tyler	Whig	April 6, 1841
11	James K. Polk	Democrat	March 4, 1845
12	Zachary Taylor	Whig	March 5, 1849
13	Millard Fillmore	Whig	July 10, 1850
14	Franklin Pierce	Democrat	March 4, 1853
15	James Buchanan	Democrat	March 4, 1857
16	Abraham Lincoln	Republican	March 4, 1861
17	Andrew Johnson	Democrat	April 15, 1865
18	Ulysses S. Grant	Republican	March 4, 1869
19	Rutherford B. Hayes	Republican	March 3, 1877

George Washington

Abraham Lincoln

Theodore Roosevelt

THEIR TERMS ⭐

LEFT OFFICE	TERMS SERVED	VICE PRESIDENT
March 4, 1797	Two	John Adams
March 4, 1801	One	Thomas Jefferson
March 4, 1809	Two	Aaron Burr, George Clinton
March 4, 1817	Two	George Clinton, Elbridge Gerry
March 4, 1825	Two	Daniel D. Tompkins
March 4, 1829	One	John C. Calhoun
March 4, 1837	Two	John C. Calhoun, Martin Van Buren
March 4, 1841	One	Richard M. Johnson
April 4, 1841	Died During First Term	John Tyler
March 4, 1845	Completed Harrison's Term	Office Vacant
March 4, 1849	One	George M. Dallas
July 9, 1850	Died During First Term	Millard Fillmore
March 4, 1853	Completed Taylor's Term	Office Vacant
March 4, 1857	One	William R.D. King
March 4, 1861	One	John C. Breckinridge
April 15, 1865	Served One Term, Died During Second Term	Hannibal Hamlin, Andrew Johnson
March 4, 1869	Completed Lincoln's Second Term	Office Vacant
March 4, 1877	Two	Schuyler Colfax, Henry Wilson
March 4, 1881	One	William A. Wheeler

Franklin D. Roosevelt

John F. Kennedy

Ronald Reagan

	PRESIDENT	PARTY	TOOK OFFICE
20	James A. Garfield	Republican	March 4, 1881
21	Chester Arthur	Republican	September 20, 1881
22	Grover Cleveland	Democrat	March 4, 1885
23	Benjamin Harrison	Republican	March 4, 1889
24	Grover Cleveland	Democrat	March 4, 1893
25	William McKinley	Republican	March 4, 1897
26	Theodore Roosevelt	Republican	September 14, 1901
27	William Taft	Republican	March 4, 1909
28	Woodrow Wilson	Democrat	March 4, 1913
29	Warren G. Harding	Republican	March 4, 1921
30	Calvin Coolidge	Republican	August 3, 1923
31	Herbert Hoover	Republican	March 4, 1929
32	Franklin D. Roosevelt	Democrat	March 4, 1933
33	Harry S. Truman	Democrat	April 12, 1945
34	Dwight D. Eisenhower	Republican	January 20, 1953
35	John F. Kennedy	Democrat	January 20, 1961

LEFT OFFICE	TERMS SERVED	VICE PRESIDENT
September 19, 1881	Died During First Term	Chester Arthur
March 4, 1885	Completed Garfield's Term	Office Vacant
March 4, 1889	One	Thomas A. Hendricks
March 4, 1893	One	Levi P. Morton
March 4, 1897	One	Adlai E. Stevenson
September 14, 1901	Served One Term, Died During Second Term	Garret A. Hobart, Theodore Roosevelt
March 4, 1909	Completed McKinley's Second Term, Served One Term	Office Vacant, Charles Fairbanks
March 4, 1913	One	James S. Sherman
March 4, 1921	Two	Thomas R. Marshall
August 2, 1923	Died During First Term	Calvin Coolidge
March 4, 1929	Completed Harding's Term, Served One Term	Office Vacant, Charles Dawes
March 4, 1933	One	Charles Curtis
April 12, 1945	Served Three Terms, Died During Fourth Term	John Nance Garner, Henry A. Wallace, Harry S. Truman
January 20, 1953	Completed Roosevelt's Fourth Term, Served One Term	Office Vacant, Alben Barkley
January 20, 1961	Two	Richard Nixon
November 22, 1963	Died During First Term	Lyndon B. Johnson

	PRESIDENT	PARTY	TOOK OFFICE
36	Lyndon B. Johnson	Democrat	November 22, 1963
37	Richard Nixon	Republican	January 20, 1969
38	Gerald Ford	Republican	August 9, 1974
39	Jimmy Carter	Democrat	January 20, 1977
40	Ronald Reagan	Republican	January 20, 1981
41	George H.W. Bush	Republican	January 20, 1989
42	Bill Clinton	Democrat	January 20, 1993
43	George W. Bush	Republican	January 20, 2001
44	Barack Obama	Democrat	January 20, 2009
45	Donald Trump	Republican	January 20, 2017

Barack Obama

★ PRESIDENTS MATH GAME ★

Have fun with this presidents math game! First, study the list above and memorize each president's name and number. Then, use math to figure out which president completes each equation below.

1. James Monroe + Calvin Coolidge = ?

2. Calvin Coolidge − Andrew Johnson = ?

3. Calvin Coolidge − James A. Garfield = ?

Answers: 1. John F. Kennedy (5 + 30 = 35)
2. Millard Fillmore (30 − 17 = 13)
3. John Tyler (30 − 20 = 10)

LEFT OFFICE	TERMS SERVED	VICE PRESIDENT
January 20, 1969	Completed Kennedy's Term, Served One Term	Office Vacant, Hubert H. Humphrey
August 9, 1974	Completed First Term, Resigned During Second Term	Spiro T. Agnew, Gerald Ford
January 20, 1977	Completed Nixon's Second Term	Nelson A. Rockefeller
January 20, 1981	One	Walter Mondale
January 20, 1989	Two	George H.W. Bush
January 20, 1993	One	Dan Quayle
January 20, 2001	Two	Al Gore
January 20, 2009	Two	Dick Cheney
January 20, 2017	Two	Joe Biden
		Mike Pence

WRITE TO THE PRESIDENT

You may write to the president at:

The White House
1600 Pennsylvania Avenue NW
Washington, DC 20500

You may email the president at:

www.whitehouse.gov/contact

★ GLOSSARY ★

administration—the people who manage a presidential government.

autobiography—a story of a person's life that is written by himself or herself.

cabinet—a group of advisers chosen by the president to lead government departments.

debate—a contest in which two sides argue for or against something.

debt—something owed to someone, usually money.

Democrat—a member of the Democratic political party. Democrats believe in social change and strong government.

economy—the way a nation uses its money, goods, and natural resources.

Great Depression—the period from 1929 to 1942 of worldwide economic trouble when there was little buying or selling, and many people could not find work.

inaugurate (ih-NAW-gyuh-rayt)—to swear into a political office.

infection—the causing of an unhealthy condition by something harmful, such as bacteria or parasites. If something has an infection, it is infected.

insurance—a contract that helps people pay their bills if they are sick or hurt. People with insurance pay money each month to keep the contract.

notary public—a public officer authorized to certify deeds and contracts, to record the fact that a certain person swears that something is true, and to attend to other legal matters.

Progressive—a member of one of several Progressive political parties organized in the United States. Progressives believed in liberal social, political, and economic reform.

Republican—a member of the Republican political party. Republicans are conservative and believe in small government.

running mate—a candidate running for a lower-rank position on an election ticket, especially the candidate for vice president.

secretary of state—a member of the president's cabinet who handles relations with other countries.

slogan—a word or a phrase used to express a position, a stand, or a goal.

stock market—a place where stocks and bonds, which represent parts of businesses, are bought and sold.

tariff—the taxes a government puts on imported or exported goods.

World War I—from 1914 to 1918, fought in Europe. Great Britain, France, Russia, the United States, and their allies were on one side. Germany, Austria-Hungary, and their allies were on the other side.

ONLINE RESOURCES

Booklinks
NONFICTION NETWORK
FREE! ONLINE NONFICTION RESOURCES

To learn more about Calvin Coolidge, please visit **abdobooklinks.com** or scan this QR code. These links are routinely monitored and updated to provide the most current information available.

★ INDEX ★